BREAKI
ARE KEEPING ME HOSTAGE

A BOOK ABOUT THE BONDAGE OF ADDICTION

Written by Cheryl Armstrong

I am dedicating this book to all those who are struggling with the bondage of addiction. I want you to know that there is hope! I can say this because I know, beyond a shadow of a doubt, that there is a way to break those chains that relentlessly and painfully pull you away from what your heart knows to be true. I pray that you will find the answers you need in order to restore your hope for the future.

Cheryl Armstrong

Peace I leave with you; my peace I give you. I do not give to you as the world gives. Do not let your hearts be troubled and do not be afraid.

John 14:27

INTRODUCTION

I believe that I am as qualified as anyone to speak about addiction and the many challenges that arise from this debilitating disease. In my personal experience, I have not only seen but have felt the ravages to mind, body and spirit that addiction can cause. I have witnessed the damaging effects to relationships, both personal and professional. Please understand that I don't want to make this a testimony about me. I am sure that you have already heard too many testimonies, whether it be in a treatment program or in various self-help groups.

However, I have worked as a nurse in the drug and alcohol arena, as well as in the behavioral health field. I have seen the hopelessness, helplessness, and despair in the eyes of those I have come in contact with during my employment.

Many have suffered the loss of their children to foster care. Most have faced a multitude of physical, social, medical, psychiatric, spiritual and legal problems. Sadly, the disease of addiction continues to increase each year. Keep in mind that addiction can take on many forms. It's not just drugs and alcohol is it? Addiction can be defined as anything that consumes us to the degree we ignore the basic needs of life; such as, food, shelter, love, and security. When our focus is strictly on how, when, and where we can take possession of our current obsession, we are unable to see the negative consequences that will inevitably occur in our lives. Sometimes the addiction can be so severe that even the risk of death is not enough of a threat to keep a person from using. Most alarmingly, death from drug overdose has doubled over the past 10 years. In 2017, it was reported by The National Institute on Drug Abuse that over 70,000 people have died.

I have worked for organizations that champion the current "cure" for addiction, but the result is always the same, relapse followed by remorse, disappointment and all too frequently, death. There is no simple "cure" for what is at the root of addiction. Mankind cannot fill the need of what is missing deep down in our souls. Man can only mask the problems.

What is the root of addiction? Well, it starts with our spiritual energy. The essence of who we are is not being satisfied. We seem to always be searching for the answers such as; "why was I born, and what is my purpose?" So what do we do? We look to the external to answer our questions, only to come up empty handed. Nothing of man will ever be able to satisfy our carnal lusts. We know this to be true. For example: we get money, we want more; we get high, then find we need more to continue to get the same feeling; one glass of alcohol turns in to two; on and on it goes. If you are serious about gaining your freedom back and no longer want to be a slave to your carnal attachments, then I urge you to continue reading.

What I am about to say, you are not going to like. Another definition of addiction can be simply put by saying; it is the act of satisfying SELF. Unfortunately, all of us are born with a carnal nature. We were also born to NEED a Savior. God has placed within our spiritual nature, a LONGING and DESIRE to have fellowship with Him. Until we understand these facts, we will continue to stay put in our prisons. When we fill ourselves with those things which are not of God, our lives will continue to feel barren and our thirsts will never be quenched.

On our own, we are not capable of giving up our rights to self; selfishness, self-centeredness, self-loathing, self-pity, etc. We haven't the power because of the fleshy bodies we live in.

When Christ died for us on the cross, He has given us free of charge, a power so mighty that we can do all things; all we have to do is access it. This powerful spirit can only come from His Holy Spirit.

So how do we gain access? It is so simple; you might have trouble believing it. But please believe it; I can give witness to its transforming and lifesaving force! First, accept, in your heart, that Christ died, rose from the dead, and now sits at the right hand of God; all to give us eternal life, and at no cost to us (that's a very sweet deal). Secondly, seek fellowship with strong and mature believers in Christ so that they can help you to grow in God's word. Thirdly, understand God's instructions for you on how to live each day by reading the Holy Bible. Fourthly, turn your thoughts to helping another person. And most importantly, pray to the Holy Spirit to help you accomplish these steps every single day.

Always remember, that we are weak in body and in mind; that we are but wretched souls and are nothing without the Lord's Holy Spirit indwelling in us. Tap into this most magnificent power and see your lives begin to change into the person God created you to be. Your life will be enriched beyond your wildest imagination. Mine has!

The rest of these pages contain poems inspired by King James Version scripture. Each of my poems is followed by a short reflection. I promise, you will find inspirational messages that will give you direction, encouragement, and hope for your future. God Bless you!

The Lord is your constant companion. Seasons and friends may come and go but the Lord is forever with you. He is there with you in your darkest hour, never once leaving your side.

BUKY OJELABI

Feeling Alone and Afraid

God has the power to help us with the
difficulties, that in our path, lays

Accept Jesus, receive His life changing
deliverance and to God give praise

Your hearts will be filled with courage, and a
new found wonder

You never have to be afraid of life, or of
being alone for you are under

God's protection, His Holy Spirit wrapped
around your heart, a part of your DNA

Thank you Jesus for the tranquility you
provide, that I can go about my day

Glad that you are forever apart of my life,
you will never leave

I have a surety of your loving presence and

power which leaves nothing to grieve

Joshua 1:9 "*Have not I commanded thee? Be strong and of a good courage; be not afraid, neither be thou dismayed: for the Lord thy God is with thee withersoever thou goest.*"

I Can
do all
through
ChRist
because he
strenGthens
mE.

FEELING ALONE AND AFRAID: A REFLECTION

When I was much younger, I often sought the "supposed" comfort of solitude for all of the wrong reasons. To begin with, I never felt a part of anything. Growing up I was very shy and self conscious about my looks and my abilities. I never felt that I was smart enough. As a kid, I was made fun of because I wore glasses, and was too fat. We all know how cruel kids can be. I was too afraid to take part in any social activity.

As an adult, I sadly discovered that isolation only breeds loneliness and fear. In this weakened state, some turn to substances to dull their senses or to feel a sense of elation. We forget or don't understand that this moment of happiness is short lived and we will be unable to avoid crashing again and again into that mountain of despair. We will continue to fall further and further away from the person God created us to be.

By accepting Christ Jesus into my heart and my life, I never have to worry about being alone. Jesus will be with me always, indwelling in my heart; continually guiding me toward the individuals who are rich in the experience of God's truths. It is this fellowship with children of God that has helped me through many trials. I no longer fear the world around me!

Anger, the Darkness that blinds

Often times in our lives we experience anger
directed towards us

People who want to derail the peace our
Lord brings, thus

Distracting us and trying to force their anger
into our minds

The unsaved person loves to hate,
producing a darkness that blinds

Blinded to God's mercy, and opening
themselves up to sin

Remember brethren that the wages of sin is
death, for when

Anger or hate fills the heart our God of love
can not dwell there

Brothers and sisters banish hate and anger
using prayer

Pray for those lost in sin and with hate in
their heart

Be slow to anger, slow to speak, and quick
to hear for love to start

Pray for the lost souls to find peace and
glorious hope

Through Jesus Christ, that they will cling to
His spiritual rope

The rope that leads to eternal life, saved
from a certain death

Pray for the lost souls that they too can

avoid that dying breath

James 1:19-20 *Wherefore, my beloved brethren, let every man be swift to hear, slow to speak, slow to wrath: For the wrath of man worketh not the righteousness of God.*

ANGER, THE DARKNESS THAT BLINDS: REFLECTION

There are many emotions we experience in our carnal bodies. A number of these emotions can hinder us from living a joyous life. In today's world, it is so easy to become angry. Often times we let these angry feelings stay inside of us; refusing to let them go. When we hold onto this anger, it continues to build into a great big ball of hate which festers and rots our souls. We are surrounded by a darkness for which joy and happiness can never dwell. It is only in the light that joy can survive.

The spirits of alcohol and of mood altering drugs will create a hole inside our hearts and our minds. This is where that ball of hate will wedge itself tightly, keeping you in darkness.

The only place you will find the life sustaining light that you need is through Jesus Christ. It was His sacrifice that gave you a way out. Only He can lift you up and out of the Evil that permeates this world, and give you hope for the future

DOES GOD HEAR ME?

God's instructions tell the believer to

continually pray

To communicate with Him not just when we

want our way

We also are to thank Him for all things good

or bad

During happy times, difficult situations too;

even if we are mad

When we talk to our Lord daily, let it be from

the heart

God may not always give us what we want

from the start

But as we pray in Jesus' name, something
begins to change

Outlooks become different, at first,
seemingly strange

Then we realize God's providence in our
lives by His design

For only He knows the future, knows what
will make us shine

Full of happiness, understanding that all of
our needs are met

We become stronger in our faith and know
there is nothing to fret

We learn our Creator's character, becoming

comfortable in His ways

Even when we don't understand, we trust in
Him and give praise

Help me oh Lord to pray from my heart with
a strong belief

Of your power and strength to banish my
weaknesses, to give me relief

From my carnal nature and the chains that
bind, giving me peace and love

A gift not deserved, but given still from my
Father Above

Thank you dear Father in Heaven for hearing
my pleas for help

Through your Son, it is the Holy Spirit I have wondrously felt

Helping me to let go of all the things I could not on my own

Your caring and merciful heart has restored me with the love you have shown

Psalm 116:1-2 *I love the Lord, because He hath heard my voice and my supplications. Because He hath inclined His ear unto me, therefore will I call upon Him as long as I live.*

DOES GOD HEAR ME?: REFLECTION

We have to fully understand the reason for Christ Jesus' death, burial, and resurrection, and to believe with all of our heart, mind, and soul that God had a plan; a plan to deliver His children from all unrighteousness, cleansing us with Jesus' precious blood. It is only then can we be assured that our Lord God can hear our cries for help. Through Jesus, we now have communication with the Father. These lines are open to all who are in alignment with God's will.

You ask, "How do I become aligned with God's wishes? First, examine all your wrongs (sins). Second, ask God His forgiveness for each of these sins. Remember, He knows your sins already; He wants <u>YOU</u> to know them. Thirdly, pray with thanksgiving for <u>everything</u> big or small, good or bad in your life. Fourthly, remember that God is our Father, and He knows what we need to sustain us even before we know it! He hears you!

God's comforting Hands

Hope is the light and faith is what can

comfort the soul

Without trust in Jesus, worldly evils will

eventually take its toll

Our hearts will become hardened and our

eyes spiritually blind

Our ears are deaf and we will carry the

weight of a heavy mind

We will be unable to hear, unable to see, and

unable to feel

God's unchanging love, His fortress of

strength that is oh so real

Believe dear sisters and brothers that God is

our one and only protector

He will provide for all our needs, from His

sweet fulfilling nectar

He will satisfy our physical body from our

nagging hunger pains

He soothes our dry and parched throats

through His cleansing rains

Always be confident in the truth that the

Lord is our sturdy rock

Have no doubts that our precious savior will

take care of His flock

So remember, believers in our Lord Jesus

Christ, to trust in Him

And be forever assured the bright light of
hope will never dim

We can have a precious hope of spending
eternity with our Master

Oh what a perfect joy to have this peace,
with no fears of disaster

I put all my trust in you, Jesus, our Lord of
Lords, King of Kings

The knowledge that you are my strength, oh,
how my heart sings

No longer do I feel a fear of falling into the pit
of hopeless despair

You promised to never forsake me and you

will always be there

Psalms 18:2 *The Lord is my rock and my fortress, and my deliver, my God, my strength, in whom I will trust.*

GOD'S COMFORTING HANDS: REFLECTION

The definition of faith is trusting in someone or something seen or unseen. It is difficult to think that something you can't see, or physically touch, can offer any kind of solace or comfort. Ask yourself, "Do you have faith that the air you breathe will sustain you, even though you can't see it?" Have you ever flown on an airplane? If so, did you trust the pilot to get you from point A to point B, not knowing the competence level of him or her? Obviously, or you would not have boarded the plane. Then there is gravity, we can't see it, yet we have faith that it will keep us planted firmly on the earth's surface.

I challenge you to stop thinking with your mind and open your heart to the truth. It is a fact that a "Higher Power" does exist, and this is our God the Father. He created the Heavens, the earth, and the universe; the vastness of which can't possibly be explained in terms of a scientific nature. Open yourself to the supernatural faith that God loves you and walks along side you, steadying you with His strong hands. He gives you the strength you need to continue on the journey that He has already mapped out for you. A journey that is rich in a boldness you have never known; a journey that will be sustained by Him alone and not by anything that man can provide.

WOE IS ME!

Don't feel discouraged, children of our

heavenly father, so Supreme

When life sometimes brings discomfort or

pain and may seem

All together too difficult to withstand, too

difficult to ever bare

Always remember that we have a Father that

really does care

When we let God chisel us, peel away the

dead layers; shape us if you will

Into a vessel that can never be tarnished by

sin and know even still

That we will feel pain, sometimes immense,

as our defects are removed

Remnants of our former selves will be gone,

we are now new and improved

Into a beautiful creature that has been

carved, free of selfishness, free of pride

No longer filled with anger, or thoughts of

criticism, with nothing to hide

Instead, we rejoice in the awareness of

God's love given to us for free

When God has finished His work in us, fear

not, for He will see

A child created in His image and made just

the way we were meant to be

When I feel the tearing pain of removing self,

I know from my bondages I am free

In accepting this, I will be content in all

things and never again raging

Always wanting more, for when I look in the

mirror I will not see a face aging

But a reflection that shines bright and

perfect made from Jesus' love

It fills me completely, bursting out of the

seams, this love from above.

I don't have to fear chastening from my Lord

for I know He does it for my good

To teach me His ways, the right ways, as any

good father should

Hebrews 12:6-7 *For whom the Lord loveth he chasteneth and scourgeth every son whom he receiveth. If ye endure chastening God dealeth with you as with sons for what son is he whom the father chasteneth not?*

WOE IS ME: REFLECTION

There will be many disappointments in our lifetime. Sometimes feelings of despair, frustration, and hopelessness can occupy our minds. We have thoughts that life is not going the way we imagined. Maybe people close to us have hurt us, whether intentionally or not.

We live in a world that can seem so hostile, with most everyone focused on surviving. Don't give up. If you will only let the Lord work in you, you can find yourself calm in the midst of all the chaos that surrounds you. God will mold you into someone you were meant to be, a beautiful and loving person; into someone where discouragement has no place; into a person who feels nothing but contentment, and is thankful for all things.

Let the Lord Jesus' Holy Spirit reside in you and not the spirits of this evil world. God's Holy Spirit will take over to guide you and sometimes chasten you. When this happens, understand that it is because our Heavenly Father wants what is best for you.

Do You Trust God or the World?

Do we let our human constraints tie us to

this world of corruption?

Do we accept defeat and risk an agonizing

separation, or a disruption

Detached from a life-giving connection with

our true and only defender?

Do we risk losing the warmth of God's love,

His awe inspiring splendor?

Or do we fight the good fight and trust in the

Lord to give us strength?

He gives us power to pull free of these

bindings and run the full length

Of the course He has designated for us that
fulfills His beautiful plan

Believers, God is with us so nothing can
break us, not even the wiles of man

Some may feel insecure and too weak,
unable to put up a fight

Instead going with what seems easier;
hiding in the dark away from the light

Giving up to swim with the current that
ultimately leads to destruction

By not relying on God's power, they fall
victim to the world's seduction

Others may feel the need to know the

unknowable depending on science

Only nothing will be clear, not until we

surrender and have total reliance

On God for He knows us intricately to the

last detail, knows what's best

He is our protector, our rescuer, watches

over us so that we can be at rest

Philippians 4:13 *I can do all things through Christ which strengtheneth me.*

DO YOU TRUST GOD OR THE WORLD?: REFLECTION

I cannot tell you how many times I have put my trust in people, places, and things, only to be knocked down to my knees. This created in me a wall of indifference. Because of this wall, any love I felt towards others was superficial at best. Happiness would appear only fleetingly. I would keep a safe distance from anything I felt could hurt me, not wanting my wall to crumble around me. I wanted to stay insulated and isolated.

Oh how wrong I was! Isolation opens the door to harmful substances that dull the mind and the senses, foolishly thinking that this will keep all the emotions we don't want, at bay.

Blessedly, I discovered that by turning to Jesus with all my heart and accepting Him as my Lord and Savior, He gladly gives me His strength. I can feel again with a joy so deeply embedded in me that all I can do is smile! My mind is clear, and my eyes are wide open with the visions of everlasting life standing before me!

The Gift of Eternal Life

What a miracle, all the blessings that God

lovingly and willingly gives to us

Yet as people born of the flesh, we will very

often continue to fuss

"Why can't I have that", or "Why is this

always happening to me"

Forgetting the promises of salvation God has

given to us for free

Eternal life that is undeserving, for in

holiness everyone will fall short

So take this gift seriously, it is not a joke, a

game or a sport

We have not earned this gift, for it is given

through God's good grace

So have faith believer and happily rejoice,

for God has reserved us a place

That is more beautiful and glorious than

anything we will ever see

A home to look forward to, filled with such

love, we will shout with glee

Once we have reconciled this truth in our

heart and not just our mind

Unending peace, happiness, and no fear of

death we will find

May we never forget this reward and our

faith never falter

Turn your life over to Jesus and place all

your worries on His alter

Ephesians 2:8 *For by grace are ye saved through faith and that not of our ourselves. It is the gift of God.*

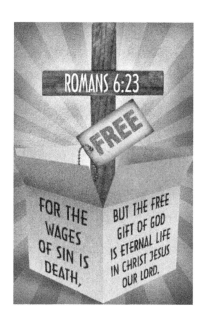

The Gift of Eternal Life: Reflection

There was a time in my life that I was afraid of dying. I thought that I would no longer exist after death and that was frightening. The thought of no longer being able to hold my loved ones or see them ever again, was to me, unbearable.

Even though I had accepted Christ Jesus at a young age, I really didn't understand the meaning or the amazing depth of eternal life. I was still a "baby" Christian, eating soft food. It wasn't until I was older that I started to grow spiritually. As I studied God's Holy Word, I began to understand the true meaning of salvation. I knew then what an awesome gift that has been given to me from my God the Father.

I can never stress enough how important it is to study the inspired Word of God. Its purpose is to show us how to live righteously; glorifying His name in everything we do and say. His words also provide comfort, encouragement, and the assurance of life everlasting. This alone takes away the fear of death. I am made strong by Jesus' love which gives me hope for the future. When I keep my focus on God alone, I am free from all of my carnal bondages.

OF FAITH NOT ASHAMED

Troubles & hardships help us to learn to live

our lives with patience

Gives us the ability to fight difficulties

without too many frustrations

These trials help us to trust in God's power

and to gain a wealth of expertise

And an understanding of Jesus that comes

to us as easy as our ABCs

With this comes hope; A hope that becomes

strong and can never die

For our loving God speaks the truth, He will

never tell us a lie

The hope of everlasting life, for this we will

not, cannot be ashamed

For we have a heart filled with love that we

have wondrously claimed

Through the cleansing and saving blood that

was shed by Jesus our Lord

In believing this immutable truth we will

obtain our glorious reward

Even though we have sinned and fall short of

the glory of God

Let the blood of Jesus wash over you and

prepare to be awed

God has proven His love for us, there can be

no doubt of His love so immense

By a cost so unimaginable, a cost taken out
at Jesus' expense

So don't be fooled by what Satan would have
you believe

The prince of lies wishes to keep you in your
sin, only to confuse and deceive

Satan rejoices by creating a world filled with
uncertainty and fear

Let not Jesus' death be in vain, hold all that
is true dear

Don't give Satan the satisfaction of securing
you in his awful grip

Share Jesus' Holy name to all with no shame

and from the Devil's hold you will slip

Romans 5:5 *And hope maketh not ashamed; because the love of God is shed abroad in our hearts by the Holy Ghost which is given unto us.*

OF FAITH NOT ASHAMED: REFLECTION

Have you ever been in a situation when someone mentioned the name of Jesus, and the room suddenly went quiet and was filled with a nervous energy? I have. It was as if a really bad word was spoken. Suddenly, everyone seemed uncomfortable. Sadly, I too was uncomfortable and afraid to stick up for my Lord Jesus. My only thought was, "What will people think of me?" When I look back on that particular event, I am ashamed of my lack of action to boldly defend the name of Jesus. The JESUS who loved me so much that He willingly died to save me from Satan's grip!

Happily, today I am no longer ashamed of my faith; for if it were not for my faith, I would be lost in the dark world of drugs and alcohol, doing Satan's bidding. After all, our carnal nature is hell bent to do the things that satisfy our selfish nature. If it were not for the Holy Spirit indwelling in me, guiding me to study God's word, and showing me the importance of fellowship with others in Christ, I would be plummeting in a downward spiral towards damnation.

Satan's lies would still be deceiving me by ringing true in my ears.

Thankfully, I have been given a purpose in life and that is to glorify Jesus' name unashamedly. I submit to Jesus and let Him, alone, control my life. You too can have a purpose in your life, moving away from despair. All you have to do is let Jesus be your pilot.

THERE WILL BE NO FEARS

It is impossible to count all those that live

their lives in fear

Being afraid of things living, and more

terrified of death so near

Fearful are the lost, confused, uncertain, or

those gone astray

From our Lord's loving embrace, their

hearts hardened as clay

But by trusting the truth of Jesus' life, death,

and resurrection

We can live bold and courageous, knowing

God's perfection

For God's obedient children have the
promise of life eternal

Our bodies, all that is physical, and
everything external

Will pass away and turn to dust, for they are
considered temporary

However, our souls are immortal through
Jesus' blood; no need to be wary

Instead we can live joyfully and in glory;
engulfed in Jesus' brilliant light

We have no more pain, no more darkness,
never again having to fight

"Are you afraid of death? No", the Christian

says without doubt

"Would you like to know why; learn what it is all about?"

The Lord is with you and sustaining you through all your life's stages

A truth that is undeniable and has been passed on through all the ages

Psalms 23:4 *Yea, though I walk through the valley of the shadow of death, I will fear no evil: for thou art with me; thy rod and thy staff they comfort me.*

THERE WILL BE NO FEARS: REFLECTION

We live in a world that is full of confusion, causing us uncertainty and doubts. With these negative feelings comes anxiety and fears. We become afraid of life and afraid of death. Those who, deep inside, feel alone in the "universe", often times turn to anything that will mask their hopelessness; hoping to get away from it all, or to just "veg-out".

I can sincerely tell you that I have found a better way. My faith in Jesus Christ and the knowledge that He has defeated death turned my hopelessness into hope; my despair into overwhelming joy. The more I study the scriptures, the more I have come to realize that Jesus is my Rock, my Comforter, and my Counselor. He is available to me 24/7 because He walks with me always. This feeling of knowing that I am never alone brings me such serenity, and when I share His good news, I feel a beautiful and glorious high of which there is nothing else that can compare to this wonderful feeling!

SOARING HIGH ON LIFE

When I fully trust in and rely solely on my

heavenly Father

I begin to feel a freeing peace, for me, there

is nothing to bother

Even as a sinner, Jesus loves me, there is no

hate or judgement at all

I feel a profound joy embedded in my soul as

I answer His call

He takes away my worries, removes my

selfish lifestyle

He gently nudges me out of myself causing

me to smile

For when my focus is on others, my heart
bursts with love

Loving all those around me, even the
unlovable; loving my creator above

My once tepid spiritual attitude turns to a
burning desire

To please my Savior with a faith so strong
that I am on fire

When I trust in God, not in some things, but
in all things

I can't be brought down; I soar high with
spiritual wings

Feeling wondrously blessed because Jesus

has restored me

To the beautiful creation that God intended

for me to always be

Ephesians 1:3 *Blessed be the God and Father of our Lord Jesus Christ, who hath blessed us with spiritual blessings in heavenly places in Christ.*

SOARING HIGH ON LIFE: REFLECTION

It takes a lot of hard work, practice, and time to give up my right to self. Some will ask what does that mean. It means to stop being selfish, self-righteous, and full of self-pride. The more I get to know Christ Jesus, the more I see it is not all about ME. Once I accepted that He is in control of all things, I am more aware of becoming a new being. No longer is my motto, "What about ME?"

It has been through God's loving nudges that my eyes are beginning to focus on others instead of my own self-pity. No longer am I looking through a haze of drug induced self-loathing. I am now gloriously high on Jesus' life giving salvation, soaring ever higher towards the destiny that God has planned for me.

God wants all of His children to feel His love and to extend the same kind of love that Jesus had shown, towards all those around us. When we can do this with the help of the Holy Spirit, we will be right with God. We will know the peace of God.

Love and Forgive My Enemies? That's Crazy

It is easy to be nice to a person who is

lovable and kind

But to the unlovable we pretend not to see

them, become blind

A challenge it is to be kind to those whom

are difficult to love

Even so, as Christians, we must heed the

words of our Lord from above

And remember that our heavenly Father

hath forgiven the saved

He has promised everlasting life, a way to

heaven He has paved

Because we have sinned time and time

again, often straying from God's path

We deserve nothing but Hell's burning flame

feeling God's wrath

But because of Jesus we are forever

pardoned from a death sentence

Know these facts to be true and always have

a heart of repentance

A forgiving attitude towards all is the way to

a tender heart

For the lovable and the unlovable, it will

become easier to do your part

So please be kind, loving, tender, and your

life will be filled

With peace abound and you will find yourself
always thrilled

To meet each day surrounded by God's
loving essence

Feeling His magnificent power, His glory,
reveling in His presence

Again I urge you, forgive, and to each and
everyone be tender

You will glorify the name of Christ, living in
His light and splendor

You will receive a rejuvenating energy filling
you with the strength you need

To conquer your demons and to heal your

soul; your heart will no longer bleed

Ephesians 4:32 *And be ye kind one to another, tenderhearted, forgiving one another, even as God for Christ's sake hath forgiven you.*

Love your neighbor as yourself. MATTHEW 22:39

LOVE AND FORGIVE MY ENEMIES? THAT'S CRAZY: REFLECTION

When we let our bondages control our lives instead of God, whether they be to drugs, alcohol, the quest for wealth, or the seeking of lusts in all its forms, we end up on the road to destruction. It is only a matter of time before we will crash and burn. We will never be at peace, nor will we ever feel joyously free. Instead, anger takes the place of love, and violence takes the place of peace.

I can look back on my life, before I truly handed over the reins to Jesus, and see that I was a hot mess! For example; if anyone dared to challenge me about something I did, I would almost always retaliate. I hated the world and everything in it. But now with Jesus by my side, surrounding me with His love, I see that ugly side of me diminished.

Just the other day, someone had approached my husband and I without any provocation, ranting and raving that we were disrespectful to the pedestrians in the parking lot by speeding. We were baffled because this simply was not true. We hadn't been going any faster than maybe 2 MPH. But because the Holy Spirit reminded me that I am to be a peacemaker and I am to turn the other cheek, I apologized and walked away. The situation was immediately defused.

Amazingly still, I felt a love towards the two men who were evidently looking for a fight. I was in awe because this simply was not me! The old self would have jumped right into a fight. Obviously it was God's Spirit in me that allowed me to love the unlovable and to rise above adversity.

Stop trying to do things on your own; it won't work now, nor will it ever work because we are our own worst enemy. Turn over the driving to one who is mighty and powerful; to the one who created us and knows every single detail of our minds, body, and soul. God wants to be behind the wheel of your life. I promise you that He is a superb driver and He will never steer you wrong!

FACED WITH GUILT

As one of God's children I try to be an

example of righteousness and purity

Understanding the sacrifice our Lord has

given, His faithfulness my surety

But born of Adam's blood, I possess a sinful

body and mind

I fail many times, for the things I don't want

to do, I do, become blind

To the things I should do, at times lacking

the determination necessary

To do what is right in God's eyes, to be holy,

therefore I must never tarry

To daily confess my sins to the Lord so that I
may be formed

Into a new and wonderful creature, forgiven
and cherished, warmed

By God's loving embrace, comforted,
protected, feeling secure

Understanding that I am forgiven for the
past, present, and future; made pure

By Jesus' blood, His unselfish suffering, His
unyielding love for the sinner

For all have sinned; Oh dear Lord, I confess
now so that I can be a winner

Of the good race, fighting with all my might,

awarded the truth Jesus told

Then barriers are lifted giving me access to

your kingdom that shines as bright as gold

1John 1:9 *If we confess our sins, He is faithful and just to forgive us our sins, and to cleanse us from all unrighteousness.*

FACED WITH GUILT: REFLECTION

There will be times in our lives when we will feel unworthy; often times feeling guilty about something we shouldn't have done or maybe something we should have done. Satan would love for us to dwell on these feelings! We will always be unworthy for God's loving mercy and grace, yet He loves us so much! All we have to do is tell Him why we are feeling guilty and He is just to always forgive us. God knows our sin nature and He knows the struggles we have. God will never tell you that you are worthless.

Satan loves to paralyze us with negative feelings so that we will be useless as soldiers in Jesus' army. Any thoughts of hopelessness, despair, and uselessness come from Satan's camp and are not of God. Always remember that Spiritual Warfare is between Satan and our Lord.

When you accept Jesus into your heart, He becomes your defender. The more your eyes stay on Him, the more you are made stronger and no longer can Satan's bondages rule your life. Profess Jesus as

Lord and join His forces. Your life will forever be changed as He molds you into a vessel of hope, love, peace, and deep abiding joy!

HOLD YOUR TONGUE

Lord Father, I need your strength daily to
hold my tongue

To fight my sin nature to participate in the
slinging of smelly dung

Talking about others, their personal lives,
what they may have done

Help me be an example of your love,
showing that to gossip is not fun

The tongue can cause much pain and is as
sharp as a two edged sword

It harms friendships, destroys one's trust;
these are not of the Lord

Remind me Father that to speak against

another is to unfairly judge

Gossiping is to be foolish and can cause one

to hold a damaging grudge

The Lord is just, I too will be examined and

not in a very good light

Dear Jesus, bring me out of the darkness,

help me shine bright

Help me to lift up and glorify your name by

being trustworthy

Keeping confidences secret, Lord I know

that I will never be worthy

Never deserving of your love, but help me to

be a witness to your grace

To be kind always in actions and speech in
every circumstance and place

I think about pieces of wood that cannot
burn without a fire

So do rumors subside without gossip, let me
be one to inspire

Being temperate, truthful and honorable
staying away from scandal

Helping to illuminate God's path with Jesus'
dazzling spiritual candle

I myself am not capable of such acts of
goodness and self denying

It is only through the awesome power of your

Holy Spirit that keeps me trying

I pray Lord for you to help me to live my life

meek and humble

Help me to realize that without you my

world, my life would crumble

Ephesians 4:29 *Let no corrupt communication proceed out of your mouth, but that which is good to the use of edifying that it may minister grace unto the hearers.*

HOLD YOUR TONGUE: REFLECTION

We have all heard the saying, "Loose lips sinks ships." I believe we all know how true this is. We also know how very hard it is not to criticize another. I don't care how good a person is, inevitably, we end up thinking something that may not be too nice. We were born in a depraved state, this is who we are. But with the help of The Holy Spirit we can keep hurtful thoughts to ourselves.

Now the enemy of God's Spirit, which is Satan's Spirit, will do the opposite. Harmful thoughts will pour from us and be spoken out loud. Face it, we have all been there. Feelings are hurt and relationships destroyed. Some will ask, "If I have the Holy Spirit indwelling in me, can Satan's Spirit fill me?" No, but we can distance ourselves from the restraining power of the Holy Spirit.

We separate ourselves from the Lord's power when we let the Spirits of Satan control us. In other words, when we are consumed by drugs and alcohol, or the things which are not of God, we are letting Satan win.

GET OUT OF YOURSELF

As a child of God and a believer in Christ's

saving power

Are we not drawn to think of others, not just

sometimes, but every hour?

Every time when we help those in need we

walk in God's light

We will be out of ourselves when we

encourage others to shine bright

We are lifted up high when lending a hand

and comforted in turn

By those we mean to support, a meekness

and humbleness we learn

We become more Christ-like for these characteristics describe Jesus

We are content in all things; it's no more about what will please us

There are some who believe they are saved through good deeds

That they will not go to heaven, so they must help those with needs

They forget Jesus' saving blood; forget that His blood is sufficient

It is good to help others, but don't let the right motives be deficient

Do it with the right heart; we help to thank

our Lord for His sacrifice

So we lend a hand and tell others of how

Jesus paid the price

Through His suffering and death, but then

from the dead raised up

To redeem us as His own so we too can

drink from His life giving cup

Of sweet nectar, the food that feeds our

body and our souls

Fulfilling God's purposes in the story He has

written, living our roles

As we live in step with the plans our Father

God has planned for us

We will be right with Him and feel His

wonderful Gladness, plus

All the blessings of comfort, guidance, love,

and a peace that can't be beat

For nothing man-made can compare with His

power to calm, nor His love so sweet

1 John 3:17-18 *But whoso hath this world's good, and seeth his brother have need, and shutteth up his bowels of compassion from him, how dwelleth the love of God in him? My little children let us not love in word, neither in tongue; but in deed and in truth.*

GET OUT OF YOURSELF: REFLECTION

I believe that most people will agree that an idle mind is the Devil's playground. When a person's life is empty, feelings of boredom start to arise; minds start to turn inward. We begin to reflect upon past deeds, the "what if's, and failures, or the like. Feelings of self-pity, worthlessness, or hopelessness, maybe it's all three, start to dominate our thoughts. The anguish can be so excruciating that all we want to do is blot it out.

We can never get rid of our despair with the use of drugs or alcohol. The feelings will only return ten-fold, becoming stronger and more intense than before! Our brains start to rely on these man-made substances and begin to deteriorate until there is nothing left. Boy! Satan loves that!

God did not create man to self-destruct! He created us to depend on Him and Him alone. He even gave us instructions on how to live our lives richly. He asks us to love Him and one another as ourselves; to focus on another's needs. Turn your eyes to God; learn His ways, and His truths. You won't be sorry because He gives you the strength to fight whatever demons that are trying to destroy you!

MY
heart & my flesh
MAY FAIL BUT GOD is the
STRENGTH
OF MY HEART
& MY portion
FOREVER
psalm 73:26

HOPE ETERNAL

Imagine a loving parent sacrificing his or her

only child

To save sinners, even those whose

behaviors may be wild

This is a perfect love so strong for the

undeserved like you and me

If it were not for this sacrificial lamb we

would not be free

We would be helplessly lost, feeling

hopelessly chained to our sin

We could not and would not know how or

have the strength to even begin

To loosen the chains of despair that pulls us
into the dark

So believe, know that Jesus is our Savior
and feel the spark

Of the Holy Spirit indwelling in us, creating
us refreshed and anew

This loving sacrifice brought believers
together, and is the glue

That keeps us magnificently whole, bringing
us back into the light

God's children, spreading this glorious truth
is worth the fight

What better gift than the gift of eternal life;

never dying

Shout; shout with joy, there shall be no more
pain or crying

Thank you dear Lord for this gift, for your
mercy and grace

That one day we will stand before you, in
awe of your beautiful face

John 3:16 *For God so loved the world that He gave His only begotten son; that whoever believes in Him shall not perish, but have eternal life.*

HOPE ETERNAL: REFLECTION

When I finally accepted in my heart, mind, and soul that God sent His Son to die for me so that I might have life, my world began to miraculously change.

I had professed Jesus as my Savior at the age of 12, but did I understand the meaning of complete submission to the Lord? No, I did not. It was not until I matured in my knowledge of scripture that I was able to fully submit. As I turned my will over to God, the Holy Spirit revealed to me that, Jesus died not only so that I might have life after death, but also so I can have life today. What do I mean by that? Well, I had no clue what it meant to really live a life full of joy; to experience not only peace with God, but enjoying the peace of God.

I can now feel the Almighty's life giving peace! I can tell you that this is something of which I could never have dreamed; this awesome serene feeling that surrounds me today!

Those living under the spell of drugs, or whatever carnality is holding them captive, will never be able to experience what I just have described. The world they are residing in is not living. They are the "walking dead". I know because I have been there, and done that. If not for God's long suffering grace and mercy, I would still be there. I thank God daily for lifting me up and out of that colony of "zombies", so that I might live!

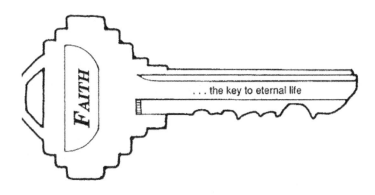

. . . the key to eternal life

Grieve No More

It is natural to mourn the loss of family,

friends, and a loved one

We can no longer hug them physically or

laugh together in fun

Feeling an ache in our hearts that brings

tears to our eyes

But let us thank God for the memories we

hold in our hearts never dies

Joyful events we can recall and think of with

affection

Thoughts of the good things, surrounding

them in a light of perfection

Struggle no more with heavy hearts for the
one that is gone

We can rejoice for believers in Christ for
they are with Him, drawn

To Jesus' home bright and beautiful,
overcoming death as He did

With a new body free of pain and deformity,
happy amid

All those gone before them, those precious
ones they adored

They now can have a glorious peace they
once could not afford

Jesus said to be of good cheer, now is not

the time for weeping

For they face no more tribulations; God's
promises they are reaping

Awaiting Christ's return, His kingdom
established sitting on His throne

A world free of evil, a place of which we have
never known

John 16:33 *These things I have spoken unto
you, that in me ye might have peace. In the
world ye shall have tribulation: but be of
good cheer; I have overcome the world.*

GRIEVE NO MORE: REFLECTION

For as long as I can remember, I knew people, (myself included), that during hardships and grief would turn to their addictions for distraction; feeling that this is the only way to cope. We would conveniently forget that this is not the way to strengthen ourselves against trials and tribulations. We forget that these bondages only make us weaker and weaker until we are but a quivering blob of nothingness. Sound familiar?

When I started turning my eyes only to God during times of sadness and difficulties, I found a strength I never knew I had. It was the Spirit of Jesus Christ indwelling in me that gave me His strength. I knew then that through Him, I can do all things. He was and is always there, beside me, sustaining me. I found such a beautiful peace that I could never find through anything else, but our Lord.

I am no longer a worthless human being. I am a person with a purpose! I am fighting the good fight as one of Jesus Christ's soldiers! I am out of my self-pity, and my mournful state. Today, I rejoice through every tribulation because I am closer to understanding my Lord and Savior.

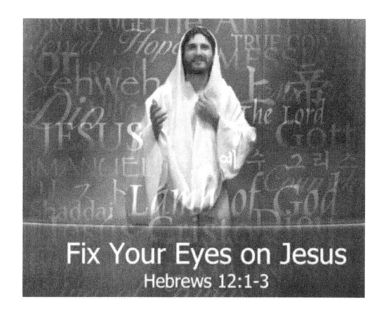

PEACEMAKERS

Anger, hatred, and resentment must be
removed from your heart

For it saddens our loving Father and keeps
us spiritually apart

Strive to live your life in peace and love or
forever remain

An orphan, separated from the Lord's family,
suffering pain

People who avoid conflicts are seen by God
in a positive light

Are deemed full of God's wisdom, for any
fool can pick a fight

When feeling unfairly treated, please don't
strike back

Always keep your temper, hold your tongue,
and don't attack

Instead pray for peace, ask for God's
wondrous strength

Ask for God's influence to hold the offender
at arm's length

Look at that person not with hate, but with
love in your eyes

Reaching out with a forgiving hand, only
then will you win the prize

That is the gift of God's mercy His Holy Spirit

a part of our soul

We can diminish Satan's grip before it takes

its toll

We become cleansed, rejuvenated, and

blissfully aware

Of God's Holy power, His protecting mercy,

and His loving care

Matthew 5:9 *Blessed are the peacemakers:
for they shall be called the Children of God*

Peacemakers: Reflection

Because of our human nature, it is often difficult to not strike back when someone has hurt us. The thought of turning the other cheek is hard to accept. Often times our carnal nature craves to seek revenge and almost all the time, it prefers to hold on to the anger and resentment. The truth is we are incapable of feeling love towards our enemies; it is only with the supernatural Spirit of God living inside of us that we can. Without it, we are powerless.

When controlled by worldly demons; consumed by the spirits of addiction, we are separated from God's powerful and loving Spirit. We will always find ourselves struggling with conflicts and we will never find complete peace. I can say this because I too have experienced a life without solace when I turned my back to Jesus.

I urge you to tap into the power that could be yours. Accept Jesus' Holy Spirit into your life. I don't know about you, but I would rather be called a child of God than a child of the sick and twisted societies within our world today. Live a life that is triumphant, a life that you can be glad to be alive and know that on God's Final Judgment Day, you will hear our Heavenly Father say to you, "Well done my child for being my faithful servant!"

NEVER FEAR PERSECUTION

My Father who art in Heaven, it is your help

that I seek

Almost always I feel so alone, wrongfully

hated, and weak

For mine enemies that are against you seem

more lively and strong

Treating me as an oddity, saying, my way of

living is wrong

God keep me strong in faith and in your

infallible word

For this is where tears will dry, my eyes no

longer blurred

Reminded of your kindness and love that
heals my wretched soul

Knowing I will be forever preserved, no
longer broken, but made whole

Through your glorious teachings, my thirsts
are finally quenched

Whereas those that mock me with hate and
jaws that are clenched

Will have thirsts that are never satisfied, like
drinking salt water

Thankful I am, for I am adopted into your
family, called daughter

As I write these words, I am renewed,

reminded of the joy you bring

Knowing you are here with me, walking with me, Oh, how I want to sing

Halleluiah! Halleluiah! Praise Jesus for glory is your great name!

Gone is the isolation that causes me to weep, my life never the same

I am filled with jubilation and laughing with thanksgiving

Hurry, become a believer in Christ to experience this perfect living

Take the chance now, if you haven't already, before you find it is too late

The Lord will give you the hope you need to

live a joyous life you can appreciate

Hebrews 13:5-6 *Let our conversation be without covetousness, and be content with such things as ye have: for He hath said, I will never leave thee, nor forsake thee. So that we may boldly say, The Lord is my helper, and I will not fear what man shall do unto me.*

NEVER FEAR PERSECUTION: REFLECTION

As I reread Hebrews 13:5-6, I pondered where my life is today. Tears of joy filled my eyes and my heart swelled with a love so great for my Lord Jesus Christ.

Before I totally submitted my will to Jesus and came back into His flock, my life was a mess. Instead of turning to Him for peace, happiness, and contentment, I turned to the world's seductions; specifically, alcohol, and sometimes, illicit drugs. I found myself often in a state of fear, feeling oh so weak. When I wasn't feeling fear, I was indifferent to everything around me. I see now this was no way to live.

Today, the Lord has healed my soul. He has freed me from fear and He has freed me from my weaknesses! He truly is my helper and He has instilled in me a peace and contentment in all things. I now know that I will never be alone; for Christ Jesus is with me always. I don't need or want anything that this world has to offer. I am free at last, free at last!

BORN FOR A REASON

Many find themselves floundering in a sea of
uncertainty and doubt

Asking always, "why am I here? What is my
life all about?

Is there some kind of purpose for me? Why
was I born?"

Seek no more, for believers in Christ no
longer need to mourn

For we trust in God's Word giving directions,
teaching us the way

Talking with us through the Holy Spirit each
and every day

We can now know that God's purpose for us
is not hard at all

Some can't believe that is as simple as
answering our Lord's inviting call

To love Him with all our hearts, to lift up His
Holy name

By following Christ's loving example we can
then lay claim

To the joyful existence created while
praising our God

For this is our purpose, to need Him and by
Him be awed

To share the good news of Christ's saving

message of hope

With God's mercy and love for us, we are

able to cope

We will be able to handle all of life's

struggles, so look no more

Be content as you follow Jesus through

salvation's door

1 Peter 4:11 *If any man speak, let him speak as the oracles of God; if any man minister, let him do it as of the ability which God giveth: that God in all things may be glorified through Jesus Christ, to whom be praise and dominion forever and ever. Amen*

BORN FOR A REASON: REFLECTION

As I sit here thinking with a clear mind, free from mood altering and mind numbing substances, I can see how easily I once fell into the trap of carnality. I was only looking to please myself and I didn't give a second thought to others around me. The further I fell, the further I became ensnared, captive to my own lusts. Contentment, what is that? Funny how the more we look for pleasures, the more we think we need. Our thirsts seem to never be satisfied.

Honestly, if it were not for Jesus and His inviting call, I would still be living an unsettled life. If I had not answered Him, I would never have discovered His purpose for me. Thankfully, I finally opened the door when He knocked! God has freed me from all of the things holding me down. I don't have to fruitlessly search anymore for the reason I was born.

I lift up the name of Jesus and praise Him daily for directing my path towards righteousness and toward His glorious Kingdom! I can't thank Him enough for sacrificing His only begotten Son for me, I am such an unworthy recipient of this, His most precious gift.

WEARINESS OF MIND

There are times when I feel an unexpected

weariness of heart

A dampening of spirit; tired of fighting

Satan's many fiery darts

These are the times I need and must

remember God's favors

To bless His Holy name with all my soul, for

He never waivers

I must praise my Lord for everything all day,

every day

I will be cleansed from within, shining bright,

lighting the way

Christianity is not always easy, and can be
gloriously hard

But I know God will not let me faint, instead I
am on constant guard

Difficulties will only rouse me to fight and
without fear defeat

The things which would have me cowering in
the dark, and I will meet

Head on the frightening storm that brews in
the back of my mind

This tempest that tries to ruin my spiritual
condition, and wants me blind

To all of God's wonderful blessings and His

loving face

Some will turn to drugs or drink, sadly this is
so often the case

Their spiritual maladies will remain for which
they are afflicted

Gaping wounds will not heal and they will
only become addicted

To Satan's harmful remedies instead of
God's healing powers

So submit always to God and revel in His
fellowship that is ours

For which God gives willingly to those who
love and obey

I love you Lord with all my soul, please help

me to never stray

Help me to remain in your good and just

graces so I may always

Have constant fellowship with you and my

eyes to you I will forever raise

Psalm 103:2-3 *Bless the Lord, O my soul, and forget not all His benefits: Who forgiveth all thine iniquities, who healeth all thy diseases.*

WEARINESS OF MIND: REFLECTION

I have discovered that when I take my focus off God the Father, my spiritual energy starts to sag. My mind begins to turn inward to whatever turmoil still resides there. It is this sin nature that I was born with that tries to take over. I start to dwell on old emotional injuries or think about the wrongs or regrets in my past. Instead of creating a positive energy, I am smothered in a negative one.

I thank the Lord that He has given me the discernment to understand that this is Satan trying to separate me from God's loving embrace. I now know that it is part of the spiritual warfare that takes place when we enlist in Jesus' army. When this happens, all I have to do is turn my eyes back to Jesus and all that He did for me; He will do the fighting for me.

Dear friends, when you find yourself weary in heart and mind, don't turn to the things of man. You will find yourself too weak and discouraged to fight the urge to hide in the darkness. Instead, submit to Jesus so that He can reside in you. He will help you to regain your strength so you can enjoy the warm sunshine again.

God gave us the instructions we need! Study His word, find fellowship with others in Christ, and Help others in need. You will never have to feel like hiding in the shadows of sin ever again. Besides, you can't hide from God. He is omnipresent and He knows everything that you did and will ever do. He even knows the number of hairs on your head!

Be still and know that I am God
-PSALM 46:10

Surrounded by Light

Jesus Christ is the only light bright enough

to guide our feet

Towards God's chosen path where our

hearts can blessedly beat

Triumphant and strong in the righteousness

that is Christ Jesus

When we acknowledge him and seek Him,

He will see us

We will be filled with the Holy Spirit which

removes all uncleanness

He washes us from our impurities, and the

weaknesses

That chains us to all that is in the world

instead of spiritual things

So acknowledge Him so you too can rejoice

in all that He brings

Understand no worldly light can completely

remove the despair

Which is the utter darkness created by sin

and is an evil snare

By which Satan entangles us with the lustful

wants of the flesh

Follow Jesus, and live! Become brand-new

and blissfully fresh

He promises us the light of life and not the

darkness of death

Oh how sweet his promise, so uplifting that it takes away my breath!

John 8: *12 Then spake Jesus again unto them, saying, I am the light of the world: he that followeth me shall not walk in darkness, but shall, have the light of life.*

SURROUNDED BY LIGHT: REFLECTION

I have emphasized the word *submission* in much of my poetry and my reflections because it is such a vital part of living a victorious life. Before my <u>total</u> submission to the sovereign power of the Lord Jesus Christ, I had been submitting my will to the world and its attachments, becoming a feeble slave. Deep down I wanted to be a "good" person, but I found myself doing the things I shouldn't and not doing the things I should. In the past I let Satan pull me into conforming to this world's views. I had let him put the notion in my head that it was far easier and better to go along with the crowd; whether right or wrong. I was weak and wanted to be liked by all. However, many times I would find myself all alone, lost, and afraid in some dark and unfamiliar place. This was no way to live!

If this story hits you too close to home, come join me into a place that is full of light, love, and comfort; a place of rest and hope for the future; a place where you will never feel cold and alone. Turn your life and will over to the supernatural love and power of Jesus. Let

Him embrace you as He guides you into His perfect light. His might is far greater than any power in this world.

Weary No More

When we turn our lives and will over to our
magnificent Lord

Oh how sweet, to feel God's life giving, life
sustaining, spiritual cord

Wrapped around us, through us, and in us,
there is no better fate

So we must always seek God's guidance,
and then wait

Without Jesus' protection and love, we are
nothing but hollow

With Him we are everything, It is because of
this that after Him I will follow

He is our strength, our protector, our hope, and our life

He helps us to soar on high with strength even through strife

So God's children, you can walk or run without feeling any fear

Your lives can now be without worry; experiencing a life here

That is filled with much joy, peace, and full of God's blessing

No more uncertainty, no more "what ifs", no more guessing

So God's children, you will walk or run with a

renewed vigor

You will have a faith that grows daily bigger

and bigger

Isaiah 40:31 *But they that wait upon the Lord shall renew their strength; they shall mount up with wings as eagles; they shall run, and not be weary; and they shall walk, and not faint.*

WEARY NO MORE: REFLECTION

It took me a while to figure out that I could do nothing on my own. My mind, my spirit, and my body were without strength. Whenever I tried to dig myself out of some mess that I caused, I only succeeded in making things worse. I would sink further and further into the quicksand of hopelessness. The world, my friends, and even my family had neither the power nor the strength to drag me out of my pit of despair. My fleshy chains continued to pull me further and further downward.

These past few years, I have felt a lovely strength and confidence in my life. What has changed? Let me tell you; it has been fellowship with my Lord Jesus, fellowship with my Christian sisters and brothers, studying God's word daily, my church, and lastly, my service to others that has changed my life for the better. I feel myself growing closer to the Holy Spirit's strength inside me. We can do all things through Christ Jesus. I can't ever imagine moving away from Him ever again and losing God's wonderful strength that helps me soar through life's many challenges.

DON'T ASK WHY

Have you ever asked yourself, I know I have

many times, why?

Why do terrible things happen that make me

so sad that I cry?

To me, just a mere human, it is impossible to

understand

How a helpless child is hurt or why such evil

roams in the land

I can never comprehend, for my ways are

not His ways

For I know I will never know the events of the

following days

My mortal thoughts are restricted to a

limited time box

But my great Father lives in a vast space

with no locks

He knows everything and has a perfect plan

already worked out

My true God is like no other, oh so

magnificent; I must never doubt

I must faithfully trust in my Lord and live in a

worthy manner

And like Him, show mercy and love to all,

lifting high Jesus' banner

For my God, my creator, is all mighty; a

powerful force

I would be a fool to rely on any human or

earthly source

I must have a supernatural faith in God's

ultimate plans

Allow myself to surrender completely into

the Lord's loving hands

Isaiah 55:8 *For my thoughts are not your thoughts, neither are your ways my ways, saith the Lord*

Don't Ask Why: Reflection

Before my feet were firmly rooted in the things of the Lord, I couldn't cope to save my life. When adversity arose, I was powerless to handle it calmly. I would turn to things I thought would make me "feel better". Little did I know that this only made my ability to handle tough situations nonexistent. I just continued to dig a hole where I could hide my head. It is so easy to make lame excuses for turning to our "vises" for comfort: "I'm hurting", someone I cared about has died", "my feelings are hurt", "society has let me down", "I lost my job"; on and on it goes.

A weight was lifted off my shoulders when I finally made the heartfelt and informed decision to submit my will entirely to Jesus, my Lord and Savior. I trust Him completely now and I can lay all my cares and worries at the feet of His Cross. He takes care of all my troubles in His way and His time and because of this, I find my wants and my needs have changed. I have no need to turn to those things of the flesh. I have a mighty Father in Heaven who knows me intimately. He knows me more than I know myself. He knows my every need and I trust that He will never forsake me! This knowledge provides me with such a glorious feeling!

Come, be a part of Christ's family, so you too can feel His loving and sustaining power!

trust in him at all times

No Need for Worry

Often times it is hard not to worry about a

circumstance or a thing

Wondering what if, asking how will it go?

What will the next day bring?

Is it something that can be changed? Well

then, change it

With the Holy Spirit living within us, we can

do all things, can't quit

Is what troubling you and bringing you

concern, out of your control?

Then place it in God's hands, for to worry is

not your role

God clothes the grass of the fields, would He do not the same for you?

Our Father knows what we need, before we were born He knew

Jesus has told us time and again through His infallible never changing words

To trust in Him with all things, remember the fields and the birds?

Our needs will be fulfilled above and beyond; needs we did not know

No need to worry; recall Jesus' promises. Be quick, don't be slow

Declare Jesus as your savior and the God of

peace be with you always

Surrounded by a warmth so exquisite

created by His loving gaze.

Matthew 6:30-31 *Wherefore, if God so clothe the grass of the field, which today is, and tomorrow is cast into the oven, Shall He not much more clothe you, O ye of little faith? Therefore take no thought, saying, what shall we eat: or, what shall we drink? Or Wherewithal shall we be clothed?*

No Need for Worry: reflection

Have people told you to "just stop worrying"? That is easier said than done, right? At one point in my life, I had little or no faith at all. I can remember describing myself as a "worry wart". I could not stay focused on the moment. My mind would continually wander off thinking about the "what ifs" of tomorrow. The more I worried, the more anxious I would become. I needed something to "chill me out". So what did I do? I turned to the only thing I knew, my old carnal ways. The end result was that my worrying mind had only intensified. When would I ever learn?

One day I heard the saying, "Worry ends where faith begins". I grew up knowing about God and how He sacrificed His only begotten Son so we can have eternal life; I had even accepted Jesus as my Savior as an adolescent. Sadly, my roots remained above ground, and I fell away from the church. It was not until I started reading and studying scripture that my roots took hold again. It was the help of my Christian sisters and brothers that helped my roots grow stronger and in turn, my faith began to grow too. My worries became less and less until they no longer ruled my life! It is such a wondrous and marvelous thing that I want to share it with all who will listen.

What is in My Future?

During the day, do you find yourself focused
on past misdeeds?

Or is much of your time spent on worrying
about your future needs?

If you are a believer in our Lord Jesus Christ
you must understand

Through His blood we are given assurances
of His protective hand

He is our loving Father now and we are His
cherished born creations

Our Lord will banish our enemies whether it
is people or nations

In our time of need for today, not in the past,
or future, but now

Draw on God's good grace, His promised
mercies, you ask how?

Simply by praying always, calling upon our
Lord for His direction

By trusting in His undying love and to Him
our personal connection

I pray for all those who don't know Jesus as
their savior and Lord

For they will never feel safe from harm from
the enemy's sword

The unsaved will live lives full of

discontentment, never to be satisfied

Fears, worries or concerns will continue to grow, appearing magnified

Christians, think not of tomorrow, stay only in the moment and trust

Hold His hand, never let go for His mercy is always Just

Hebrews 4:16 *Let us therefore come boldly unto the throne of grace, that we may obtain mercy, and find grace to help in time of need.*

WHAT IS IN MY FUTURE?: REFLECTION

It is so hard not to think about what tomorrow has in store for me. It has taken daily practice to keep my thoughts in the here and now. Some have asked me how I keep myself from thinking about the future. My reply is simply, through daily prayer; for it is the Holy Spirit that gives me faith. He helps me to understand that nothing is in my hands. It is impossible for me to know what will happen the next day, so why worry. My husband has a saying, "The past is history, the future is a mystery, and the present is a gift from God". Let's enjoy today, for the Lord of the Universe has given this day to us. Don't spend your time in fear and worry. Fear and faith cannot occupy the same space.

My husband and I try to start each and every day by reading God's instructions for us through His inspired Word that is contained in the Holy Bible. We then offer up thanks to Him for His wondrous works and we pray for those in need. We don't listen to the news or read the newspaper, which so often times, only report the negative events that are happening today. In the evening, before going to sleep, we review our day. We then ask God for His forgiveness for our sins. We ask Him to help us to do better tomorrow. In doing these few steps, we have found that our focus has shifted from ourselves to the things of the Lord. No longer do we feel the world's anger, resentment, uncertainty, and doubt crowding into our lives.

This definitely works for us. I don't know if it will work for you, but you won't know until you try it, right?

CHRISTMAS, A TIME FOR JOY

There will never be a day past, present, or
future that can compare

In His magnificent importance, a day that we
can declare

A Savior has arrived, a most beautiful and
loving gift from God

He was born perfect, holy, sinless, all
mighty, never flawed

Our Lord was born into the flesh, and was
made unto man

That He may know our personal struggles
which was part of God's plan

For Jesus to take our troubles, our

transgressions upon His shoulders

So we may be freed from the burdens of sin,

and become shareholders

In life everlasting, becoming a part of our

Father's loving and peaceful empire

Away from the turbulence and violence,

souring ever higher

Towards the comforting bright light that is

the arms of our deliverer

Rejoice, be giddy with glee, and for your

sake, don't become a lingerer

Accept Jesus into your Heart and into your

life before it's too late

To experience the great joy that is this gift

from God; please don't wait

Would you have peace and happiness

abound, forever flowing?

Then without hesitation, without doubt,

possess the certainty of knowing

That God's plan provided a child named

Jesus unto us was born

To ensure His children remain blameless

and perfect, never to mourn

So this Christmas season, rejoice in what

God has given

So that we can be made righteous through

His Son and our sins forgiven

Isaiah 9:6 *For unto us a child is born, unto us a son is given; and the government shall be upon His shoulder; and His name shall be called Wonderful, Counselor, The Mighty God, The everlasting Father, The Prince of Peace.*

CHRISTMAS, A TIME FOR JOY: REFLECTION

Oh what warmth and comfort I feel in my soul when I think about God giving me a Savior. Born was a child by the name of Jesus who was destined to take upon His shoulders all of my burdens. He didn't come for those thinking they are righteous and He didn't come for the healthy in spirit. Jesus came to heal the sinner. I'm so glad my Lord came for me to cure me from what ails me from within my spirit and soul. My healing took some time, but with Jesus' soothing balm, I finally feel a spiritual fitness for which I have never known.

Growing up, my childhood was tumultuous at best. Often times I felt unloved. My siblings and I had a stepfather who did not hesitate to show us that we were unwanted and hated. If we didn't do something to his liking, we were slapped around. He felt kids were not to be seen or heard. He especially hated my older, developmentally challenged, brother. Many times my brother would be locked in his room for hours on end. He was not allowed any games, books, or TV. to occupy his time, so I would sit outside his door to keep him company. We would play cards, slipping them underneath the door.

When I finally grew up and left home, I would feel a hot rage come over me whenever I felt provoked. Now whether this was a result of nurture or nature, I don't know. What I do know is that Jesus has calmed this rage in me. It has disappeared! Our Lord can and will perform miracles in our lives. He has the power to transform us!

I can never thank Jesus enough for being my Healer, my Comforter, my Rock, and my Everything!

Happy Birthday!

HOPE ABOUND

The special day that is called Easter, is a day
of celebration

A day to rejoice; delivered for our offenses
and saved from damnation

Our sins are forever banished by Jesus'
atoning sacrifice

What a love so pure that He would spill His
own blood to pay the price

He willingly died a horrific death so that we
may be spared

God's wrath and to continue to live; there is
no doubt our Lord cared

Cares for us still; remember the penalty for

sin is eternal death

But believers in Jesus shall not perish,

singing praises with every breath

Jesus died, overcame the fires of Hell, and

Had victoriously risen

To reign over us forever, giving us a way out

of our sin prison

Hallelujah, I shout. What a time to smile, a

day to hold dear

For on this day our Savior has risen to

banish death forever; that is clear

Help others to smile this day, and tell them

Jesus' story

Give them hope so they too may share in all
of God's wonderful glory

Romans 4:24-25 *But for us also to whom it shall be imputed, if we believe on Him that raised up Jesus our Lord from the dead. Who was delivered for our offenses, and raised again for our justification.*

HOPE ABOUND: REFLECTION

The more I became entangled in the chains that bound me to the things which caused me despair, the more I felt worthless. I felt that there was no way anyone could love me for me. My heart became hardened and I built an impenetrable wall around the delicate most inner part of my heart. I did not want to be vulnerable to those who could hurt me. I see now that I was living in a vicious cycle.

Thinking about my past life gives me a grateful spirit today. I am so thankful that I was shown how important I really am and how much I am loved by Jesus Christ. Today, I no longer feel worthless. Of course, I will never be worthy of God's free gift of salvation, but because I accepted the fact that Jesus died, and rose from the dead so that I might have life after death, His Holy Spirit pierced my heart. He tore down the barriers I had created.

Now, I have a wonderful boldness and a strength that sustains me. I have a sureness that I will never again become a slave to my past bondages. Never again will I be the person I was, because I am made new in Christ! I have been given hope abound!

Old Selves Gone

If we hold firm and fast to our faith in the

awesome powers of God

This New Year and years to come, we will

know that His rod

Will comfort us and give us joy; He will wipe

away our tears

Our hopelessness will turn to hope;

eliminated will be all our fears

We will become brand new as the New Year;

old selves are gone

Gone are all things negative; we are fresh

and beautiful as the new dawn

We have a peace knowing that God is always

with us and in us

He encourages His beloved children to love

and thus

We become stronger with no more sorrow

and no more pain

It's this love that lives deep in the heart and

not in the brain

That keeps us joyously free, today,

tomorrow and forever

We are not dead in sin, but gloriously alive

because whosoever

Believes in Jesus Christ as their savior, shall

not perish but know

Everlasting life; so this New Year I hope you
will vow to let go

All former things of your old sin nature and
become reborn, oh so new

Christ will dwell in your heart so hold on to
all that is true

Thank God daily for opening your eyes and
letting you hear

So that you may always feel His love drawing
you near

To the warmth, and solace, and comfort that
you will ever need

To become whole and secure, and from the

bondage of sin you will be freed

Revelation 21:3-4 *And I heard a great voice out of heaven saying, Behold, the tabernacle of God is with men, and he will dwell with them, and they shall be his people, and God himself shall be with them, and be their God. And God shall wipe away all tears from their eyes; and there shall be no more death, neither sorrow, nor crying, neither shall there be any more pain: for the former things are passed away.*

OLD SELVES GONE: REFLECTION

Have you, like me, made many New Year's resolutions only to fail and turn back to your old ways? I cannot count the number of times this has happened to me. I tried to rely on my own ingenuity and my own strength. I was too set in my ways, foolishly thinking I was strong enough. How terribly wrong I was. Until I learned that I am nothing without Christ Jesus, I could only fail time and time again. My weakened body and mind would always succumb to the lusts of the flesh; the same lusts that would always create havoc in my life.

My friends, I wish that I would have given up my pride and completely submitted to Jesus' truth sooner. I would have been freed from the strangle hold of all my bondages a longtime ago. I could have saved myself a lot of pain, physically and mentally. I suffered needlessly with a mental anguish that was often times, so very hard to bear.

Today, I am living a victorious life! No longer do I suffer the torment of my old self!

HAVING A THANKFUL HEART

Beloved children of whom our Heavenly
Father shows a love abound

We were adrift in a sea of uncertainty, lost,
but now we are found

We never felt whole, never felt a part of, but
now we belong

We fit in with Christ's family where
contentment dwells lifelong

Where we were once full of ourselves,
prideful and self centered

God's immense love, through Christ's
sacrifice then entered

Showing us how to live our lives with a
richness once inconceivable

Giving us joy we knew not and a love once
thought unachievable

Hearts are no longer disquieted; we now
have a spirit of thanksgiving

Towards not only ourselves, but others too,
we have attitudes of forgiving

No more negativity, no more anger, no more
emptiness

Instead we are with a humble quality and a
spiritual healthiness

In this way we are Christ-like, pleasing to

God, we can boldly go to Him

Presenting our requests and be assured that
His blessings will never be slim

So be content in all things with the
knowledge we are not alone

We are surrounded by God's protecting
power; all our needs are known

Philippians 4:6 *Be careful for nothing; but in
everything by prayer and supplication with
thanksgiving let your requests be made
known unto God.*

HAVING A THANKFUL HEART: REFLECTION

Thanksgiving is a time for family and friends to get together for a time of remembrance; looking into their lives and finding things or circumstances for which to be thankful.

Some of the things that I am grateful for today are a reflection of Jesus' transforming power in me. I am so very thankful for, not only my biological family, but my church family as well. I feel so blessed to be serving the Lord through the many ministries to which He has led me. I thank the Lord everyday for the church He has found for me and most importantly, I am filled with enormous gratitude for God's inspired and Holy Word for it is through His sacred Scripture that I have been given the tools I need to live a life pleasing to God.

I have heard a lot of people say, "How can I be thankful all the time?" Of course it isn't easy and it does take practice. Like anything that we practice constantly, eventually it will become second nature.

Every day when I get up, I thank the Lord for giving me another day to breathe His air. During a rainy period, I thank Him for watering the grass and plants so that I don't have to. During the hot summer, I thank God for providing air conditioning for my home and my car. During the cold season, I am thankful to have warm clothes and heat. Be thankful for even the little things. I know life isn't always easy, but you can always find something positive to be thankful for; you just have to give it a try. Don't ever focus on the negative things in life; Satan uses them to bring you down. Negativity will always foster a discontented and unsettled heart.

Let me give you just one more example of being thankful of the little things in life: One day, my husband and I were out doing some errands and our car broke down. Instead of grumbling, we thanked the Lord that it happened when and where it did. My husband did not have to work that day and it was close to home. We could have easily griped and moaned about our situation, but because of Jesus' Spirit residing in us we are able to have a thankful heart even during seemingly times of misfortune.

With continual practice of thankfulness, one day you will realize how much more you feel contentment, until finally, you will be content in **ALL** things.

A Loving Heart

To Love each other without hesitation takes

patience and much courage

It can be hard to love without reservation

and to encourage

But when we strive to follow all of God's

examples of love

We will know the abiding joy that can only

come from above

Let us make every effort to love without any

conditions attached

For we will know a peace and contentment

that will go unmatched

So seek God's guidance, His unfailing

wisdom as you pray

I promise you that God will help you gently

along the way

For our Lord God loves each and every one

of His chosen

He has designed the heart, a perfect vessel

for love to grow in

We learn to truly love by letting God's love

into our heart and soul

With His help we can rid ourselves of hate's

ugly black hole

John 13:34 *A new commandment I give unto you, that ye love one another; as I have loved you, that ye also love one another.*

A LOVING HEART: REFLECTION

I am sure that many of you have heard the saying, "Love thy neighbor as thyself". This is one of God's greatest commandments. Out of this commandment flows a life that will reflect all of God's blessings. God doesn't mean to only love that person who loves you back, or that person who is kind. God wants us to love even our enemies! Say what! That is impossible! Yes, it is impossible by us alone. We are incapable of that kind of love without the Holy Spirit indwelling in us. By accepting Jesus Christ as Savior, we can be a part of this spiritual phenomenon.

I personally know a lot of people who are comfortable in their anger and hate. I was one of them. It is all we have ever known. Anger is an emotion that can come so easily; the effect that it creates in the brain is a "high" of sorts. Some say, "Why should I strive to love?" Because, love causes a bigger and better "high"! You feel as if you can walk on water, just as Jesus had.

Hate and anger will only cause isolation, a sickness of the heart, and a life of complete and total misery. It ages a person; turns them into something ugly, both outside and inside. Whereas, when someone possesses love, they are made beautiful. The phrase, "love makes the world go round" is so true. You will find your life becoming brighter and brighter; oh so glad to be alive!

If you haven't already, accept Christ as your Savior. You will find the strength you need to love even your enemies!

The Lord does not see as mortals see; they look on the outward appearance but the Lord looks on the heart

1 Sam 16:7

Author's Note

My most fervent hope is that this book will have some impact in changing your life for the better. As I have stated before, I know the struggles and the difficulties of everyday life. I know that without the right direction or support in our lives, we can be filled with a hopelessness and helplessness that seems endless. We can feel as if we are stuck on a track with no hope of jumping off as the train comes barreling towards us. I want to impart to you that, with God's guidance in your life, you can jump off that track of despair before your life can be wrecked any further!

I believe that you are most likely reading this book because you are searching for something to change your despair to joy and your weaknesses to strength.

Call upon the Lord. I promise you He is the answer and you will never regret your decision.

Cheryl Armstrong

ANOTHER BOOK OF INTEREST BY CHERYL ARMSTRONG

Start each day with an inspirational poem that is inspired by a scripture verse (KJV).

Before heading out into the world and facing all of life's trying challenges, relax and read an uplifting devotional.

For just a few minutes out of your day, you can change your day to one that reflects a right frame of mind; filled with a positive outlook that can better help you cope.

God provided us with His Holy Word so that we can have the right direction in our lives.

Now available at www.Amazon.com

Made in the
USA
Columbia, SC